Kentucky's Spiritual Vortex

Also by Rev. C. L. Snapp

Tomorrow Is Waiting-An Interactive Guide for Living with Grief

The Destroyer Desires Your Faith, Not Your Soul – Surviving Grief, Loss, Depression, Doubt & Loneliness

Escape from Way Station Manor

Awaken to Our Enchanted Universe

When Momma's Cry, the Darkside of Yearning; Grief after the Loss of a Child

Kentucky's Spiritual Vortex

A Sacred Journey of Love

Rev. C. L. Snapp

©2015 Rev. C. L. Snapp

Rev. C. L. Snapp, Publisher

Cover artwork: Guided Paintings by Phyllis Vaught

This work may not be reproduced in whole, or part by any means including digital for personal or financial gain.

All Rights Reserved.

ISBN-13: 978-0692456811
ISBN-10: 0692456813

DEDICATED TO:

The Voices of Truth

PREFACE

I remember when I was around ten years old, I was washing my hands in the bathroom sink when I cupped my hands, filled them with water and started funneling water down through the overflow hole, imagining a pipeline connected from my bathroom sink across country, and all the way to the driest towns in India. As I filled the hole with water, the water filled the pipeline, and at the other end of the pipeline were thirsty people capturing the water in containers. One of those silly things the imagination of young kids can dream up.

But as an adult, I often recalled this moment, and thought maybe I had missed the boat. Maybe, just maybe, I was supposed to be a Missionary, and got distracted by life.

I will be sixty years old soon, and it took this long for me to gain the spiritual understanding of my activity in the bathroom that day. Water is life. Did you know blood is ninety-two percent water, and that our brain and muscles are seventy-five percent water? Did you know seventy-one percent of the earth is covered by water?

Water is life.

Henry Ward Beecher said, "Truths are first clouds; then rain, then harvest and food."

Beecher's statement perfectly describes my spiritual journey. As a young girl, I followed the Christian faith and attended evangelical churches. Those were the clouds of Truth in my life. My life was touched by death early. My father's carotid artery exploded, and he suffered a fatal heart attack when I was eight years old. My oldest sister was murdered when I was in my late thirties, and in June 2006 the unimaginable happened. The phone call from hell. The dreaded drive to the local trauma unit for any parent. Our twenty-two year old son, a winding, tree-lined, country road, and a motorcycle.

Life as we knew it ended.

There is not one thing in your life that

is not affected by such an event, not one. The struggle became overwhelming and six years later in January 2012, I penned the poison of grief that was killing me in *"When Mommas' Cry, the Darkside of Yearning; Grief after the Loss of a Child."*

This doesn't make me an expert on tragedy or forgiveness, but it made for a perfect storm that the Universe could use to its benefit.

In June 2012, six months after I published my journey with grief, once again life as I knew it changed forever.

First the clouds of Truth, and now the rain.

As Beecher said, "Truths first appear as clouds." That is my purpose for writing this book to bring life to the clouds of Truth *behind the veil*, and because the Spirit of the Lord has asked me to. Just as John was directed in Revelation 1:9, "Write what you see in a book." So I shall.

On June 12th, 2012 around 9:30 p.m., I was walking outside our home and was taking random pictures with my Canon

PowerShot. A very simple digital camera. I became interested in a phenomena people were calling Orbs. Just a few weeks prior, an internationally known medium contacted my son during a live television show. First, my religion taught me against such activity. But fate intervened. I didn't know this man was an internationally known medium. I submitted a question for him to interpret a dream. But the Universe had other plans.

The producers of the show, nor the

medium had any of my personal information, not even my name. The information that was sent to me gave me no choice but to pursue Truth.

I was not familiar with the term Orbs, I didn't watch the popular ghost hunting shows, and in the six years since my son's crossing over, I hadn't once considered talking with a medium. I didn't go to them, the Universe brought them to me.

So, within a few weeks I was armed with my camera and asked the Universe if there was *anything* around the house that might show up in a picture. I snapped several pictures, didn't notice anything out of the ordinary. It was a beautiful warm night. The stars were out, the weather was great. I didn't expect to see anything.

I connected my camera to the computer and prepared to upload the images. I will never forget the shock, the fear, the excitement, the "oh hell" moment when images showed a huge red Presence glowing over the top of our house. This Presence could not be seen with the naked eye.

This was the beginning of a journey that continues to this day, and my work of spiritual photography. The Spirit of the Lord with the assistance of Archangel Raphael, Archangel Jophiel, and the Elders of the Most High have revealed their desire on more than one occasion that I am to "write what I see". I did share my earliest experiences in a very small book, *"Awaken to Our Enchanted Universe."* To my amazement this work has received 5-star reviews on Amazon.

During the past three years of my awakening, I became interested in inspirational writing. I have come to learn that many great novels were developed using this technique. But this is not a novel. I desired inspirational *spiritual* writing, and that is what I asked of the Universe. Many of the images that have been shown to me through the use of digital photography may not be accompanied with an interpretation of what you are seeing. I am wondering if the Universe left it this way because the images are energized, and blessed with a message specific to each individual who may witness them. Thereby, leaving the interpretation of the image to the Spirit and the individual's need.

*"**Your faith is only as strong as the test it survives.**"*

Dr. Myles Munroe

1954-2014

In this first book of a three book series, I will share many of the earliest images in 2012, and images as recent as 2015. But a great deal of the text in this book will be *Inspirational Spiritual Writing*.

I do not claim to have authored much of what you will find between these pages. I claim to have authored the book because I am responsible for the taking of the photographic images contained within this book but not the images themselves. No photograph has been altered, edited or Photoshop. The only tools used to 'reveal' what is in the photograph are the basic editing tools of contrast, lightness, and the use of cropping for a closer look. I share my journey of debunking the images, debating the professionals, and defrauding the public in my early book, *"Awaken to our Enchanted Universe."*

Interpretation of the text, and the images in many instances will be up to you, the reader.

One housekeeping note, the design and layout of this book is on purpose. It is not designed according to industry standards or other works comparable in size. It is designed with larger font, and additional spacing for a reason. The design is so the work can be digested. As with any good meal, the best part is enjoying the moment. The message is to encourage you to be you, be yourself, be original, and stop settling for anything less. Like Munroe, many religious teachers talk about a test, and most of us relate to these tests through physical, financial, even emotional trials or periods of teaching; because we all agree, there is no better teacher than experience. But do we ever consider that what we believe should be tested?

If sharing my experience, my journey with you does but one thing, I hope it will challenge what you believe. Not change what you believe, not ask you to believe what I believe.

This is to test *what* you believe, and *why*.

At noon the sky became extremely dark. The darkness lasted three hours. At three o'clock, Jesus groaned out of the depths, crying loudly, "Eloi, Eloi, lama sabachthani?" which means, "My God, my God, why have you abandoned me?"

Some of the bystanders who heard him said, "Listen, he's calling for Elijah." Someone ran off, soaked a sponge in sour wine, put it on a stick, and gave it to him to drink, saying, "Let's see if Elijah comes to take him down." But Jesus, with a loud cry, gave his last breath.

At that moment the Temple curtain ripped right down the middle.

Mark 15:33

I don't want to waste another minute. I want to know Truth, I want to meet Truth. I want to be Truth.

 ## February 10th

My prayer today was in sharing my desire to bring Truth through inspirational writing. Asking God to use me for the purpose of bringing the Light of God to the world. I began to dictate the following:

Faith comes by hearing Truth.

Fear is the Watchman at the door of Pride. Fear guards the entrance from the unknown.

Fear and Pride ride the wings of destruction and death. Pride guards the ego from criticism and judgment.

Fear and Pride are the Dark Twin Towers disrupting the life force flow. One is frozen in Fear, the other full of Pride.

Incapacitated vessels that God can't fill. Vessels full of themselves.

Dormant and lacking luster.

Fear and Pride bear no fruit.

No reproduction.

No seed.

No fragrance.

Frozen and Full.

Pride says, "I am in need of nothing." Dependent upon no one.

Pride is a self-promoter, self-provider, and self-centered.

Pride is arrogant, boasts of itself, and its accomplishments.

Pride makes no mention of others.

Pride glorifies itself, not its Creator.

Fear stands guard at the door of perception, prohibiting Pride to see its true nature.

"Breathe and let the light of God's truth reveal us to ourselves that we may be healed, restored, and renewed."

Gold & Fuchsia has revealed itself as the Essence of my oldest sister whose life was taken. A 2013 image.

 February 26th

My meditation and prayer today was to inquire of the Lord concerning a vision I had of several hands, each with a pen and pad of paper as though they were preparing to write. I dictated the following:

These are the Elders of the Most High. It is fear and doubt that has you hesitating. Fear of criticism, and fear of leading one astray. Are these not my children? Am I not capable of returning them to the line of Truth if they lose their way? How will many find their way and Truth lest they have a teacher?

You are looking for man's approval, and man's acceptance—it is imperative for you to lay aside those weights of the ego. These are but stones of destruction. Open your heart, and begin to allow the River of Life, the Truths of the Universe to flow—you have your eyes fixed on the seen, and the small area of your life—words are life! A life force and frequency that creates and changes worlds! Come

Up Higher, John—Come Up Higher!

Trust.

Lay down the guard you have, this that is known as logic. As a planner at heart you are waiting for the plan—the beginning and the ending. But the River of Life flows at will.

Get in and ride. Then write about that which you will be shown. It is not an idea or a method. It is past, present, and future—it is now.

So climb aboard, will you? Fear is a

perception.

Trust.

It is time to come out of the illusion—Come Up Higher!

One may ask, "Where do I begin, and when do I begin?"

Beloved, you already have the answers to both of these questions within you. As it is not a matter of where or when—you have already the victory. The awakening of your soul. The moment you recognized the need to ask the questions. Many fear they are unable to begin, they look back, and carry their history with them.

Many fear they cannot begin a new for fear of the future as it holds unknown questions—dark alleys, and mountains of challenge.

They feel they are no longer capable of overcoming. But Truth says both are false perceptions. Yes, it is true. You have experienced many activities in your life you call history. But it is not behind you. The experiences are not in the past but are now—your desires for the future—the thoughts you have about your future are not to be found in tomorrow, or next week, or next year.

This perception is false. Truth says your future is now. God is the same yesterday, today, and forever; He changes not.

You are of God.

You are the same yesterday, today, and forever. You change not. Yes, it is true. Your body, your physical shell changes—yes, it is true your environment that you see, and experience around you changes. What we are referring to here is your life source.

Your being.

It is this life force—the being within you that awakens to the Truth. With this awakening comes the power needed to escape the Great Illusion.

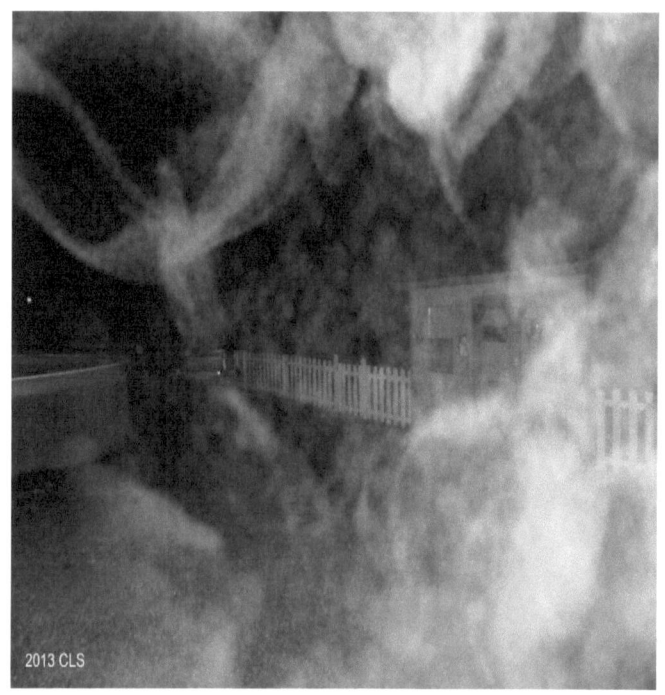

Insight by Thomas Freese

An incredible amount of Spiritual Energy appears in the above image. I titled this my "Holy Spirit Dove" photo and is to the far left of the image. Thomas Freese provided great insight with the revelation of the Griffin. Multiple Griffins in flight but one clearly visible to the far right of the image. When I shared this information with my husband, he immediately suggested I take a look at our Coat of Arms. After doing just that, my response to Tom's insight; you simply can't make this #!@* up! The confirmation was astonishing. My husband's Coat of Arms emblem is the lion, and my emblem is the eagle. Why is this noteworthy?

The Griffin is thought to be a legendary creature with the body, hind legs, and tail of a lion; and the head and wings of an eagle. There are no coincidences.

In antiquity, the Griffin was thought to be a symbol of Divine Power and a guardian of the Divine. Clearly the Griffin is not a legendary or mythical creature.

Lion and Eagle—Coat of Arms—Spiritual Vortex. Enter the days of technology.

Many different teachings offer the theory of the veil is thinning, or lifting. But Mark, chapter 15 describes the veil ripped from top to bottom. No more separation from God, the Life Source, the Creator of everything.

February 28th

My prayer and meditation intention today was to allow the Elders of the Most High to speak. The following is my dictation:

The delusion of the masses has caused great sickness to the very source that supplies the life source. Many are asking why so many are sick, what are these ailments that our families suffer.

It is a manifestation of your own self-serving delusion. The core relationship between humanity and the planet, and the well-being of both is love.

When humanity began loving themselves, and their achievements—the reciprocation of the path for love—the life source for your planet; the planet began to suffer. Her very activity to this day is responding to the lack of love from that which she gives life.

She becomes withdrawn, and her pain flows through the ash of the volcanoes. Like a woman in travail, pining for her child—estranged and lost; she rests not.

The lack of her rest is added pressure to the ecosystems. The life source she provides to sustain life is now at risk.

Case in point—the nuclear plant in Japan. The wastewater is poisoning not only the planets inhabitants but as one who would attempt suicide to escape the pain, she is now suffering from the slow death of poisoning.

Cause and effect is not a cliché'. It is not a simpleton phrase. As your physicians utilize radiation to rid one of disease; children of the Most High; children of the Light—you must begin to radiate your love to the one who loves you! The One who nurtures you, feeds you, and shelters you.

A mother in travail. A mother filled with despair. Can you not see? Will you not turn?

Pivotal!

Lay down your weapons of war. Lay down your weapons and submit to the Most High.

Pivotal!

There will be no healing for humanity—there will be no cures for what ails you. These gifts shall not be released to you for you have shut up your bosom. You have no concern for the One by which you live. Like leeches, you draw from her resources, you rape and pillage her grounds. Then you turn, and stuff your waste into her womb. You have covered her face with asphalt, and sealed her pores with concrete.

She is barren.

Pivotal!

You must reconcile with the dust from which you came. Break open your glass houses. Allow the healing love of the Most High, to radiate through you as you reconnect with the One from which you came.

God spoke, "Let us make human beings in our image, and make them to reflect our nature. They can be responsible for the fish in the sea, the birds in the air, the cattle, and yes, **Earth itself.**"

Wind of Change—appeared when I prayed about Chemtrails in 2013.

He said, "All that has been and all that shall be resides within me."

C. L. Snapp

Appeared during a prayer of Forgiveness (Top)

Image taken April 2015

 March 1st

My prayer and meditation today was to seek authors of Truth who reside in the Light. The following is my dictation:

Everything begins with one.

One thought, one desire, one hope, one wish, and one good deed.

One soft word, one smile, a single rose petal, a gentle spirit, a cool breeze, The Beginning, One.

The tapestry of the web of a spider begins with a single anchor point. Today, cast off the anchor of bitterness, un-forgiveness, and entitlement. Anchor yourself to love, and the cares of this world will vanish. Your eyes, your ears are gates leading to the soul. Gates by which you are fed.

What you are reaping is that which is being sown into your soul. The seeds of hate and division—seeds watered with lust, greed, and control.

It is time for you to set a watchman at the gates of your eyes and ears that your soul may be nourished by that which is beneficial to the good of all.

You suffer lack, war, and destruction as a result of your diet. Your suffering is but a reflection of what you have ingested. Change your diet and suffering shall cease.

The hunger for death and destruction is as the vessels the widow prepared for the prophet. The oil ceased when the vessels ceased. As it is with death and destruction.

The hunger for such must cease. The rise in darkness, the depth of despair is attributed to the overwhelming desire for constant information. The nonstop flow of toxic information.

Idle words spewed nonstop. No rest for the vibrational frequencies of your planet. Constant information of no value, spewing into the souls of humanity—as it is with the waste in your nation's landfills. Noise pollution is a great enemy.

Many run from silence. But it is in silence you will hear the voice of the Most High. It is at this time of silence that you will begin to remember.

To remember the Master Key to your future. To know the purpose for your life. To recover the precious stones you have carried with you on many journeys.

The power to remember will be found as you seek Truth above all else.

Many will attempt to block Truth through false teaching, false doctrines, and false promises—even the most Elect of God will be deceived.

Your battle begins the moment you question. But it is this recognition to question, that will lead you to the Light of Truth.

As it is with the planted seed—the first struggle is in the darkness, isolated, and hidden. It is in this struggle of the seed to break through its cocoon, its shield now to find a greater struggle facing it to rise through the crusted soil—shifting dirt, and gravel as it struggles toward the Light.

Then dependent upon those who nurture it with water and fertilizer—protection from disease, and predators. As the young seedling rises from the deep, darkness from where it was planted. It rises above the struggle *with* the very dirt where it was planted, and begins to find its footing and strengthens—growing even taller toward the Light. Now dependent upon nature to pollinate it blooms that it may produce fruit. It all begins with one seed.

One.

But the level of success of this seedling is reliant upon many factors.

Water.

Protection.

Pollination.

Then, as the pollination takes place, and the fruit appears, this is the victory. For the fruit is a life source for others. Seed time and harvest.

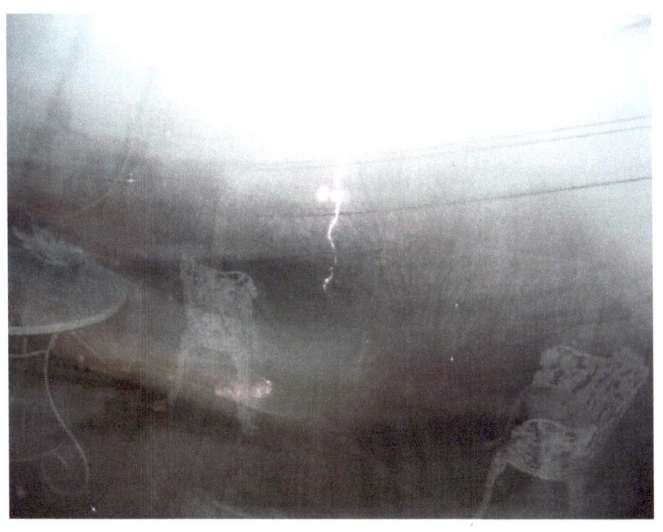

Lightning and Energy – not taken through glass.

Image taken April 2015

The irony here in this photo and your interaction with the spirit realm is that this photo could be titled "Through the Looking Glass" as you are like Alice in Wonderland, entering a realm of greater spiritual contact, helpful communication and being available to pass along both process (how you have been given these photos) and product (the pictures themselves). Like Alice, you have fallen through the rabbit hole and you'll never be the same again, no matter what the mundane world of physical reality says is real versus what is derived from imagination. You are a living example that "the medium is the message" that not only are these photographs a vehicle for contact but you yourself are a portal that attracts this very process. We all have access to the magical/spiritual realm to *better understand the greater matrix of grander spiritual reality and so that we may turn to Spirit and each other to help all who come to God with an open heart and mind.*

The jagged lightning bolt down the middle of this photo represents the Biblical tearing of the Jerusalem temple veil itself (at the crucified death of Jesus) that symbolically separates common reality from the sacred. See Matthew 27:51 "And, behold, the veil of the temple was rent in twain from the top to the bottom; and the earth did quake, and the rocks rent". And you yourself have undergone a crucifixion like experience with the loss of your son; but out of that experience you have found your true self, a self that cannot be shaken, that is fully sympathetic to anyone you encounter, and that as mentioned above has taken you beyond so called normal reality, or perception of same, into the very nexus of creative spiritual reality.

Yet even these amazing photos are but one level of evidential phenomena that may pass in time as you are able to perceive all these energetic beings and talk with them without requiring a sort of proof of their existence. Blessed are those who have NOT seen and yet believe, and there *are greater visitations for you that will only be seen with the inner sight of spiritual reality. Be confident that your work to share these photos with the greater world will give hope to many. And of course, there will always be those who "have not eyes to see" no matter what is presented to them in good faith. You have angels around you and they consider you their equal…so rise to every challenge you face with a pleasant knowing—you are blessed and no apparent separation such as we call death is permanent or could ever draw us away from our loved ones.*

Thomas Freese

C. L. Snapp

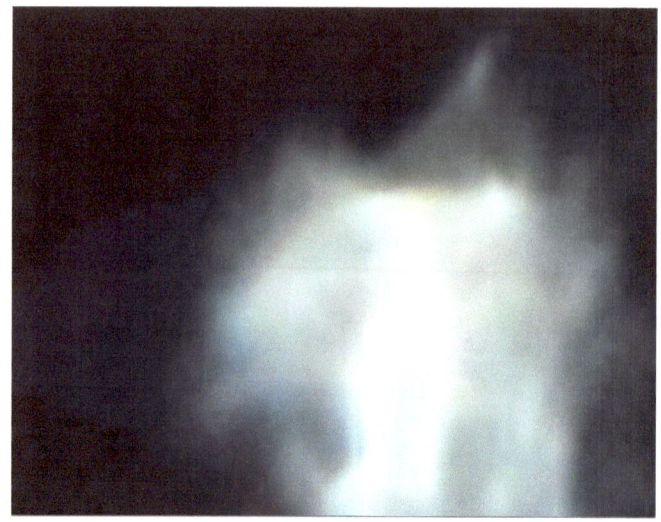

The Blessed Virgin Mary (above)

Images taken July 2013

And the true irony is Tom began his insight on the photo above with an analogy of the Alice in Wonderland adventure through the looking glass. In the story, one of the characters is a Gryphon, though in the story he is the opposite from what legend had recorded about the Griffin. There are no coincidences.

 March 6th

I recently had an amazing discovery in the Book of Revelation. John describes the rainbow. Not a rainbow as you see in the sky after a storm, but a rainbow that accompanies the Divine.

In Revelation 10:1, John describes what he saw. He saw an angel coming down out of the sky. The angel was clothed with a cloud. A rainbow was on his head. His face was like the sun, and his feet like pillars of fire. Now take another look at the image of the Blessed Virgin Mary. Do you see it? Do you see the rainbow above her head, and clothed in a cloud? The very center of her presence as bright as the sun.

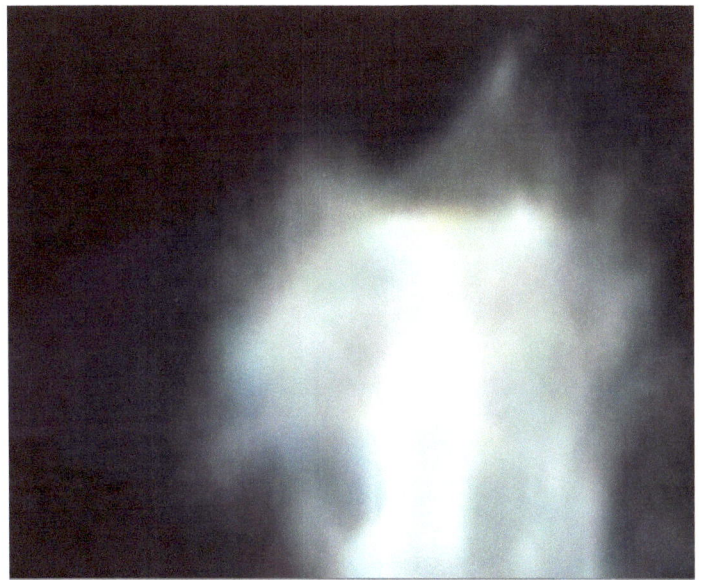

During meditation the words *"Are You Ready?"* appeared in white on a very large board. I dictated the following:

We, the Elders of the Most High are thankful for the willingness of your Spirit as you continue to reach into those unknown areas of guidance and wisdom.

We, the Elders of the Most High find great encouragement in your desire not to settle for the path of ease—the path well defined so many travel. It is with your desire, and hunger to know Truth, and to know God that brings us to you. For few are chosen is but because few seek.

God is not sparse with his Keys to the Kingdom. What loving father conceals gifts from his children forever?

What would it benefit the Father of all to withhold the very keys necessary for his children to proceed?

As one who seeks, and arrives at a gated location—a desire to continue the journey to see what is there. Yet, you are unable to obtain what you are seeking without the key to proceed.

This would be considered tempting and teasing. Our gracious Father is neither a tempter nor a tease.

It is His greatest desire that His children achieve all that He has placed within them.

The keys to unlock all that is within you is found in the seeking. The search for Truth is a diamond in the Crown of Life. The diamond that generates the power of life and illumination.

The greater the desire in the search, the greater the illumination. God is no respecter of person.

The illumination of wisdom is in direct response to the level of desire in the search.

For one who desires greater and deeper illumination, one need to deepen the purity of desire in the seeking.

As God knows the intention of the heart. He knows the motivation driving the desire. One's desire should remain pure, and honest to the empowering, and goodness of all mankind.

This illumination is not given to one who has not yet tamed his pride or who continues to feed off of his ego.

Though a great desire for illumination would be driven by these. But the search never breaks through the secured gates, and falls back to the darkness of the heart, bringing with it the weight of selfishness by which it was released.

There is nothing new under the sun—many generations have attempted to put simple truths in new packages.

But it is not the glitz of the wrapper that you are seeking. It is the Truth within the wrapper. This is proven by watching a young child unwrapping a gift at Christmastime.

The gift is inside.

The value is inside.

Yet more times than not the multitudes of young children will be entertained by the bow, the wrapping paper, and the tape.

Discarding with little attention to the perfect gift purchased in love by their parent. As it is with the Father's children. He has wrapped each, and everyone in a unique wrapper, and as children no matter their physical age, be it two, twenty, or sixty-two—they spend much of their life's energy playing with, and focused on being entertained with the wrapper in which He placed specifically chosen, and valuable gifts.

Yet, more times than not these gifts are discarded with little or no attention given to them. And as it is in the natural, many gifts require additional effort for them to function.

Some may require assembly. Building. Some may require batteries. Power. Some may require learning how to use them. This is also true with the gifts our Heavenly Father has placed within you.

Many will begin to recognize their

gift—suspect there is a gift, but do not want to invest in the additional time, and effort; do not wish to labor in the assembly or in the finding of the power source, or investing the time to learn how to use this gift.

So the gift remains untouched.

Dormant.

Discarded.

And as it remains, decay begins to erode, and this decay comes in the form of un-forgiveness, bitterness, resentment, fear, doubt, criticism, judgement, and hopelessness.

Even the finest, purest silver when discarded becomes tarnished. It is time to take eyes off the outside wrapper—the size, color, sex, it is time to turn off the voices of the world. These are but the money changers. And it is time to discard the childlike ways of playing with the vessel which was birthed, and focus on what the vessel contains.

This awareness is the greatest gift you

can give to mankind. Without this, all your efforts, your motions for a better life, a better community, a better world are but clouds without rain.

Motion but no change.

Movement but no life.

Kentucky's Spiritual Vortex – A Sacred Journey of Love

And without altering the integrity of the photo here is another look at the photo of the large Presence in front of the house. Using filters to peel back the layers of light, or dark in the image.

Now take another look at the Presence in front of the house. Do you see him? Clearly there is a life form within this Presence.

 April 6th

Coming into the still, small, quiet place—where the machine stops, the wheel stops, and I get off for just a few minutes.

A time of acknowledging a Divine Source for everything, simply acknowledging, and to say thank you.

Hearing the silence of Life.

The tangible presence of Love.

Welcoming the Love, and the Light

of His creation.

Recalling Scripture—unless a man leave, walk away from, separate from others, wife, mother, father…this is the key to finding the Divine that lives, and loves through you. As humans, it is our nature to be social—to feed off of the interactions and accolades of others.

A good dose of medicine for the ego, but not for your soul. Your soul yearns for the opportunity to separate, to be at one with the Divine.

Unless you leave, separate. It is a Spiritual Key to the Kingdom. This was not meant for celibacy in the physical, though, rightly so, the Divine may call you into a season of denial—it is a "Come Up Higher" moment—to leave all the busyness of life behind—be still, listen, and wait.

Soul reflection—a mirror opportunity with the Divine Source living within each of us. This time of reflection brings wisdom, guidance, direction, peace, comfort, and healing.

These are the jewels one should desire to adorn themselves as they prepare to interact with others throughout their day.

Separate from the daily grind, the earthly demands, even your own physical desires come away to the Secret Place—to be one with your Creator.

C. L. Snapp

no street lights
no moon
simply Majestic

2013CLS

A g84

 April 13th

I wait. I have come again to this quiet place. The sun is high in the sky—I pondered over the Charles Dickens writing of May 13, 1827. Finding adventure in each new day, he writes

So I wait. Wait for Wisdom to come, and to speak. I dictated the following:

Wisdom has spoken reminding me of this early morning, welcome, Wisdom was speaking to me about suffering.

"Suffering travels on the Wings of Truth," says Wisdom. It is through suffering a person comes to know Truth.

Truth about themselves.

Truth about life.

Truth about death.

Truth about love.

In my discussion with Wisdom, I asked if it was necessary to suffer in order to obtain, in order to know, in order to become aware of Truth.

Wisdom was quick to point out the free will of a person's soul.

If one chooses the way of love above all else, one need not suffer to know Truth.

"Love above all else."

All.

Everything, including yourself.

Then Wisdom reminded me of the teaching of Jesus—Jesus was aware of and had known Truth before his suffering on the cross. Yet, he goes one step further and shows us that Truth can also be found on the other side of suffering.

Choose this day.

The way of Life and Truth.

Then love above all else.

To choose frustration, worry, anger, greed, lust, envy, hate, deceit, discord, disease, and discouragement—to choose, this is to deny love and in doing so one denies Truth and Life.

When there is Love, there is Truth

and where there is Truth, there is Life.

Jesus showed us *the* way, and used himself as an example.

I AM, the Truth, the Way, and the Life.

I AM.

I AM, that I AM.

God is Love.

Love is I AM.

Love is the Truth, the Way, and the Life.

Love above all else.

This transcending power of love is the Key Keeper for transcending the physical dimension—transcending the weights and cares of the physical world to behold the beauty of the Universe—God's Kingdom, and all that is within it.

Every living creature abides with this power. The power to create through vibrational frequencies.

Be still and know.

What do you feel deep within your

heart and soul?

Is it anxiety?

Fear?

Guilt?

Lack?

Rage?

Anger?

Hate?

Discord?

Doubt?

If it is any of these emotions you are feeling then this is what you are pulsating throughout the Universe. You may see it on the local news, and the internet. When you see these images, be still and know, begin to recognize these thoughts and actions in your own life, and make a choice—begin to choose; Love above all else.

Above your personal desires.

Above having your way.

Above being right.

Above being first.

Above your perceptions.

You can start by being still if just for a few seconds, and focus on your breathing—when you focus on your breathing—you don't have thoughts racing through your mind.

Another place to start may be the next time you have to wait in line for something—be still inside—breathe, and connect to; Love above all else.

C. L. Snapp

This Energy Vortex image taken Memorial Day 2013.

 ## April 16th

Why is it when I feel most compelled to write—I struggle the hardest—my mind spinning—my thoughts scattered?

I write from research—I write from experience. But I AM writing from inspiration.

I want to let the waters of Living Water to flow through me. I AM not a writer, I AM but the tool. The pen. A vessel used by a Presence much larger, much greater than myself, than me.

So, I ponder on the author of the novel eerily written before the sinking of the Titanic that foreshadowed the reality of a sinking Titanic ship.

Morgan Robertson authored *"Futility"*, featuring an ocean liner that sinks in the North Atlantic in the month of April after striking an iceberg. Robertson wrote the novella *fourteen years* before the Titanic tragedy. At the time of his writing, the Titanic had not yet been conceptualized. The blueprints had not been printed, the contractor had not been selected. No tickets had been sold.

I ponder on the prophecies of Nostradamus, Edgar Cayce, and Mother Shipton, and I wonder.

Is it possible—the Power of the Written Word? If the Written Word is a word divinely inspired can it fall to the ground? Or does it take on a life force, or form of its own?

Is it possible to write our way out of

disaster?

2015, the year of the Shemitah, the year of conspiracies gone wild, the year of NIBIRU, and the Asteroid; of Chemtrails, of large jetliners such as MH370 loaded with hundreds of passengers…missing in thin air. In a day when every passenger on board would have possessed a personal cell phone, and technological equipment such as iPads, laptop computers, Twitter, and Facebook. Yet, no signals, no pings, no word. No signs. Missing in thin air.

A year with talk of time travel, time manipulation, global disaster, and destruction.

Is it possible, or more yet, probable—that an inspired Written Word can change, or at least influence the future of humanity, of society as we know it, and the planet?

I contemplate the disappearance of the dinosaurs, Atlantis, the building of the great pyramids. And I wonder, if a high form of Consciousness could or would use the form of the Written Word to impact life as we know it.

I AM Revelation.

The Prophets of old were instructed to "write the vision and make it plain".

Is it possible, then, if not probable, that an inspired vision today—written in the form could, and would mold the future?

And if so, what would the vision say?

I have been trying my hand at watercolors and one day I ask the Lord to show me how he sees the Earth. I was in total shock when this was the vision. (Above)

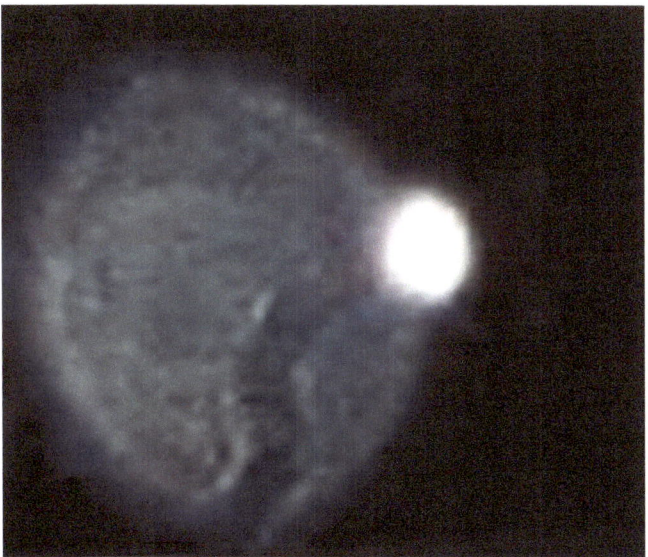

There is indeed much power in this scene, not only the visual representation of Glory but also the much more dramatic energy that overlays that which can be seen on the digital picture. In this scene we are treated to the wonderful and playful coming together of several strands of power; there are the nature spirits, the fairy folk, interacting with the orbs which, shall we say are individualized essences of the Mother God aspect of divinity as it arises from the consciousness of Mother

Earth. Skeptics will say that photographic orbs can be created from the camera interacting with dust or moisture, but who can explain the full Universe of glory indwelling each molecule and is not the dust of the earth the creative playground for the gods?

I see this scene as one of those times when something of great beauty or power can literally take our breath away. The music of the spheres takes place not only in distant space as great planets encircle our sun, but in every corner of our world and anywhere in the Universe. You were given then a glimpse of glory and asked merely to be a witness—what an honor!

These beings of nature will communicate with you if and when you dedicate yourself to channeling what they have to share. Know ye for now that the greatest love of one human for another is available in each magical moment, between any of these scintillating creatures of light and a mortal observer. Of course to use the word observer is inaccurate and you take part in the glory of the divine any time you wish and certainly as you walk outside your door with an expectation—a hope that God will speak in diverse ways, that love is a decision to participate in the dance of life, that the great experiment is simply to open our eyes and behold the wonder of creation.

Thomas Freese
Kentucky Author & Storyteller

 March 2nd

Today, I have come in meditation and drumming. I wait.

And the Rider on the white horse appeared, and he was traveling at a great speed. A great number of white doves were traveling with Him.

And He said, "Peace is coming."

As He rode, the white doves flew with Him, other riders on white horses began to appear behind Him. Other riders began to mount their horses, and join Him, and I heard Him say, "Let Peace arise." I heard Him say, "Many are waking from their sleep—many are riding."

Peace arise.

Peace is coming.

God will arise, His enemies will be scattered, and those who hate him will flee before Him.

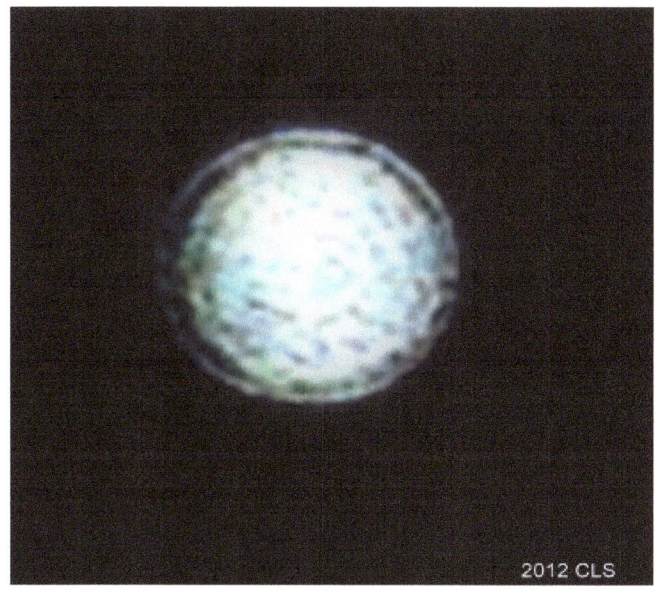

 February 4th

I approached today with meditation, stillness, and drumming. I dictated the following:

She is a great spirit of lying and deception. Her drug of choice is lust— she is a spirit of perversion, and distortion, but her greatest tool of choice is persuasion.

She is as old as the forest, and her roots are grounded into the hearts of men. She is the great deceiver as she has many faces.

In her path, she has left many victims—both known, and unknown.

She is called Death and Destruction.

Few escape her ways.

Image taken 2015 (Bottom)

 April 26th

In stillness today, I sit, and I observe nature. The sun is bright, and the sky is transparent blue. Another one of our early butterflies dropped in to feed on the lavender lilac bush today. He is dark in color with a large orange patch on each wing.

He is free. He is graceful. Today, I have come to sit among the Presence that I photographed yesterday. A brilliant pink Presence last night, photographing pink is rare. Charts have been created for identifying the meaning of the various colors that appear. Labels. Who determines the labels, and why? Red means this, and green means that. I have often wondered if the Presence I am photographing isn't a mirror or reflection of my own soul.

Crazy, I know. But what if there is some deep, unknown historical map within each of our souls? And these images are the 'movie' or 'history' of my own soul's journey.

I mean, think about it. What if it is a reflection of a soul's journey? Red means something different for everyone. Some see red as a symbol of love, as in red roses, red hearts, and Valentine's Day. Yet, to others red is considered aggressive, hostile, anger, and danger.

Society labels things that are hot, and dangerous with red. It could also be possible for red to represent passion, and desire. As with a burning desire. If in time, all come to realize and acknowledge the work of spirit photography, the unseen as a mirror or reflection of our 'true essence'; then the colors, and manifestation photographed take on an altogether new understanding.

Giving voice to Presence.

Love – The key to transcendence and transformation.

"Are you ready" is appearing everywhere now.

"Are you ready?" My answer is yes. My question is, "ready for what?" And then I hear a subtle, "change."

Are you ready for "change"?

Most of us would immediately respond with a resounding "Yes!" if not, "Hell yes!" But Truth is, change is not easily welcomed. And even more difficult to pursue, to embrace, to maintain, to comprehend, understand and accept.

Most of us, our version of 'change' is not at all in alignment or in agreement with the 'change' the Universe has in store. And when 'change' comes, and come it does; it comes as a thief in the night—unannounced, unexpected, and to the majority or the vast number of us—then unwanted!

We don't see nor consider the 'big' picture. We gaze up to the stars at night and see the Big Dipper as the Universe. The moon made of cheese—and an occasional falling star as an opportunity to make a wish.

The Universe that creates life is far vaster, far greater than what we can see.

The Universe must be experienced. One must transcend from the vessel of humanity as the butterfly transcends from the chrysalis—one must be willing to detach from what is seen—what is tangible, and say "yes" to all that is possible. Yes, to the unseen, the unknown. Be willing to travel the cosmos as you come to understand you *are* the cosmos. The cosmos dwells within you, and you within the cosmos. When you come to understand the physical realm is a form of expression—

the Universe (God) expressing itself in colors, shapes, ideas, and species; then the same life force expressing itself through the bumble bee, expresses itself through the hummingbird. A Consciousness of Love, and the Expression of Love.

Resistance-Reaction-Retaliation

Does the butterfly have any say in its length of days? A spring tulip or a day lily, both express incredible beauty after a harsh winter season—busting forth with vibrant color; yet their days short. The season of their beauty, short. Yet do they grumble, complain, or do they return next spring after remaining dormant through the heat of the summer, the brutal cold of the winter; and yet, when the Universe calls they are ready to answer the unseen call—the silent Voice, the nudge that says "prepare yourself as Spring approaches, and your day of expression is arriving."

Do we have the power to deny the call of the Universe? The One who breathes life into every living thing? Or like the spring flowers, do we anxiously await the bidding for one more opportunity of expression?

In September, the Monarch butterflies will be making their annual pilgrimage to Mexico—to deny the nudge to do so would mean certain death—death to self, and death to a species—death to expression.

"Love—the threshold to Glory."

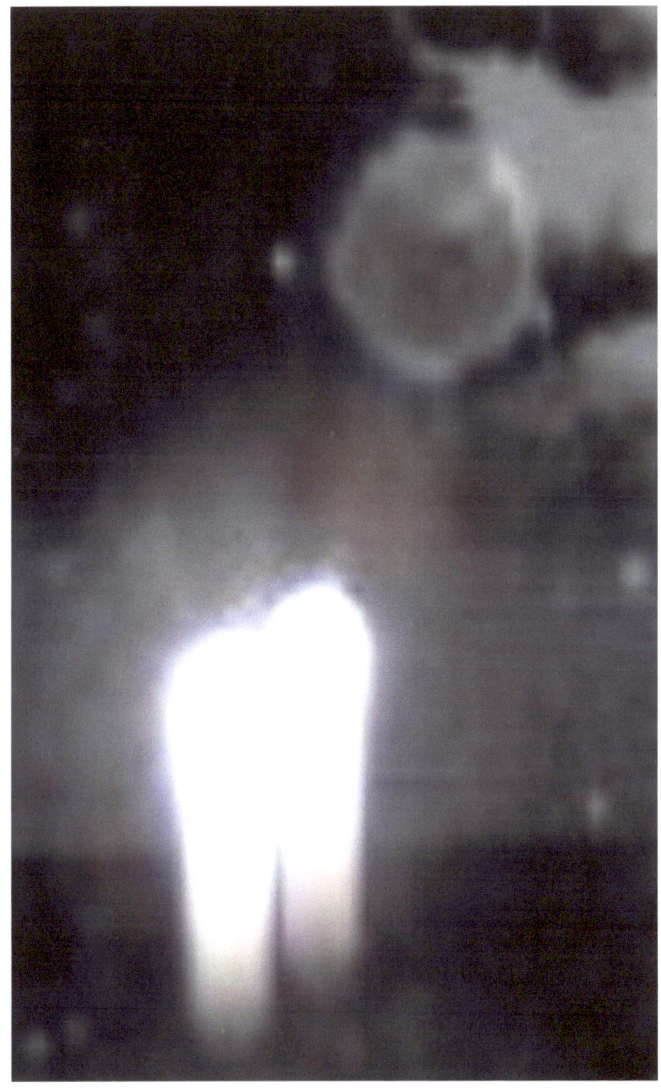

Image taken 2013

 April 27th

In meditation and drumming today, then I sit, and I wait. I dictated the following:

Love is not a man that it can be tamed, nor is it a machine that it can be driven.

Love is.

Unmeasurable.

Untamable.

Undeniable.

Indescribable.

Love is.

Love is an experience.

A journey.

Love is a refuge.

Love is currency.

The more you love, the more love finds you. Is it possible to have love for the dying rose as much as it is possible to love the bouquet of two dozen roses delivered for a special occasion?

Is it possible to experience love in the transition?

Life is transition, constant, and sometimes radical transition. Is it possible to allow the transition without resisting the flow, the direction, the change? Or will reaction, and retaliation become companions?

Building dams in reaction to the transition cuts off life support. The flow of life is diminished—the longer the dam remains in place—the greater the suffering. Emotional, spiritual, psychological, and even physical suffering will manifest. What's more difficult than the building of the dam? The dismantling of the dam in order to resume the life flow. This can happen once you recognize your role in the suffering.

The ownership.

The dismantling process will be a slower process than when you constructed it. When you built the dam in your resistance response, you had a little help from your friends; *adrenaline, anger, rage, guilt and disappointment.*

When you make the decision to dismantle the dam, it's going to be you and God. The emotions, the enablers won't be around to help. The strength, trust, and fortitude needed to recognize you built a dam in the first darn place will be multiplied during, and after the dismantling process.

In other words, once the dam is

dismantled, and you are 'back in the flow', you're not going to be weighted down with guilt, anger, rage, and disappointment; instead you will be stronger, wiser, more compassionate, more understanding, and more empathetic.

It will be this Truth and Life that brings you the strength, trust, and fortitude to keep going. A constant encourager—"This is the way."

Love is.

C. L. Snapp

A g128

 May 4th

In meditation and stillness today I wait. I wait to hear. I am a willing vessel, willing to share that others may find healing and hope. I dictated the following:

Today is the day of salvation—no one knows what tomorrow brings though there are many who forecast the future, who forecast the weather, who forecast crops, and rewards—but none know for certain.

The Creator of all things is the Source of tomorrow. But He makes no promise of it—it is the desire of the Creator that you fulfill this moment, this day with all your heart's desires, then at the end of the day, as the sun retires, you receive your reward of a job well done. Your opportunity to create—your legacy. And what will that be if tonight the morning glory departs? Have you left seed that shall never perish, but continue to give life, light, and hope? And though the morning glory does not depart but with the sun rises to one more day, one more opportunity—what will you choose to do with this gift of life? Will you invest, and nurture it, recognize it for the treasure that it is, or will you squander it away on childish matters that when the morning glory no longer returns with the dawn of a new day—will there be no residue, no seed to regenerate life, light, and hope?

These are the gifts you have always within you—they cost denial of self. They cannot be purchased with money.

Freely you have been given, and freely you should give—cast your bread upon the waters of humanity, that the earth be filled with the Creator's Glory!

Then comes the test. I leave the house and a few miles away I realize I left my phone behind. Frustration sets in, but I am close enough to turn around, and go back and retrieve it.

I turn around. About half way back to the house, I see him. The man walking on the side of the road. I saw him earlier before I realized I didn't have my phone. But I didn't stop, I am a woman alone, and had just come over a hill when I saw him walking. Timing. He was bearded, covered in dirt and grime of the earth, not of the world; and he had a small, very small backpack.

I wanted to stop, but I have offered help to others who appeared to be in need, and they insisted they were not in need, and were offended.

Not a minute had passed after I drove

past this man walking, that I realized I left my phone behind. In all honesty, it was a frustrating realization that I didn't have the phone, yet in just that quick moment, I had already forgotten about the walker. But the minute I saw him after turning around, I felt it—that thud! That thud you get in your heart when you know this is a test!

Forgotten phone.

Turning around.

Now a 'real' reason to turn around. A

lot of teachers will tell us we should never look back or go back. But had Moses not looked back—he wouldn't have seen the Glory!

I say some of God's greatest encounters are moments when we 'change direction', 'change or focus our attention'. The ability to be flexible, recognize a need for a change, and then to go with the flow.

Even the great Mississippi River flowed backwards during the 1811 earthquake. Am I any greater than the great Mississippi? Now my heart is pounding. I am an older female, alone in the car. A bearded man weathered by his current conditions. Fear of offending him. Fear of being alone. By the time I reached the house, I had decided to grab a cold bottle of water, it was for him.

So I grabbed the phone, the water, and headed back to the car. Oh Lord, I thought, send me a sign so I know I am supposed to stop when I see him. Slow the traffic—no traffic—maybe he will be resting under a tree; after all this is a major highway. Lord I need a sign that this is what I should do. I reached for my wallet, I had two five dollar bills, and two one dollar bills—no twenty.

Okay, well ten dollars is all I had, so I folded the two five dollar bills together, and laid the water in the seat. I locked the car doors, and rolled the passenger side window down.

Now I needed a sign. My meditation this morning said, "Fulfill this day with my heart's desire, and leave a legacy that reflects life, love, and hope." And within the hour there is a bearded man walking the best he could toward town. No sign of a broken down vehicle, just a very small backpack over his shoulder.

Why are the things we want to do the most, the hardest? I topped the small hill, and there he was, still walking, but obviously struggling physically. Looking in my rear view mirror—no cars behind me.

I slowed, not knowing whether I should pull off the road or just slow down. He sees me slowing down, and starting to pull over, and he walks toward the car. I have the bottle of water, and the two five dollar bills in my hand—as he approaches the window, I ask him if he would mind terribly if I bought his lunch today?

He smiles.

He reaches in for the water and the money. But I can tell you, the water was just as valuable as the money. He smiles.

He is wearing gloves with the finger tips cut out on this 70° Kentucky morning with full sunshine.

His fingers covered in grime, and his clothes showing signs of weeks, if not months of daily wear.

He smiles, he thanks me.

I tell him town is just over the hill and I pull away. I cried most of the way to work. Not because I did anything special, and not because I had enough to share; but because *he* was special.

The ying and yang of life.

The knowing there is a valley just on the other side of every mountaintop, and that God is the Source on the mountaintop and in the valley.

He smiled, I cried; and life is good.

My son, Richard. His Essence has been photographed on a regular basis for the past three years. He flies high, he dances, he laughs, and he has enjoyed every moment of this journey. I believe it is his hope, and purpose you will do the same.

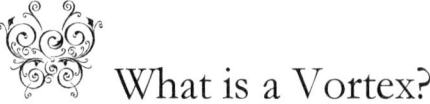 What is a Vortex?

Also known as Vortices, they are described in any online dictionary as:

A whirlpool of swirling water, fluid, or air that sucks everything toward its center. An activity, situation, or way of life regarded as irresistibly engulfing. Inescapable and destructive.

In simple terms Vortex means, *"to turn".*

To turn, what a profound revelation of Vortex. I am convinced if you were to become engulfed in a Vortex, you too would be forever changed. Ask anyone who has survived an EF5 tornado, and I'm sure they will tell you they were profoundly changed.

Turned.

But tornadoes and waterspouts are examples of physical forms of Vortex. There are also the unseen Energy Vortexes. Students of meditation will find themselves studying the history of Sedona, AZ. According to Pete Sanders, Jr, and a Sedona resident who has researched the topic for thirty-five years, Sanders states conflicting views exist on the origination of the term "Vortex". Many believe one of the earliest to use the term was trance medium, Page Bryant. The term is used to describe powerful meditation or energy sites and centers.

These unseen Energy Vortexes have to be *experienced*, which are why many skeptics call the whole thing about Energy Vortexes and Spiritual Vortexes bologna, or poppy-cock! But I ask you, how do you explain the physical sensation of a sexual orgasm? If you have had such an *experience,* you might describe the breathlessness, your heart rate, or the ecstasy of the pinnacle. But would your description be convincing enough to satisfy their curiosity, or would the *experience* be the best teacher?

If you are serious about tapping into a higher, Universal Consciousness and Awareness, then I recommend reading, *"Scientific Vortex Information-The Free Soul Method"*, by Pete Sanders, Jr.

Kentucky's Spiritual Vortex – A Sacred Journey of Love

 Tap into Kentucky

Kentucky has a rich history of Spiritual Encounters of the unexplained kind.

Kentucky Trappist Monk, Thomas Merton experienced this spiritual energy when on March 18, 1958 in Louisville, KY, he was suddenly overwhelmed with love for others. So much so, he describes the experience as seeing people walking around downtown as though they were shining as bright as the sun.

Today, the Abbey of our Lady of Gethsemani, near Bardstown, KY offers tours following in the footsteps of Thomas Merton.

Located in Bourbon County, KY is the small community of Cane Ridge. The *experience* is often referred to as the *Second Great Awakening,* when a camp meeting in 1801 drew thousands of people when the area was largely unsettled.

Sixteen miles south of Lexington is the rural community of Wilmore, KY. On Tuesday morning, February 3, 1970 a routine gathering of students and clergy at Asbury College was scheduled to last about an hour, until the *experience* that turns you around took place. A student who experienced the spiritual energy described it as an aura, a glow that filled the chapel. The service went for 185 hours non-stop, and eventually spread throughout the U.S., and impacted foreign countries.

The Energy Source is here and is waiting for someone to tap into it. Merton, Cane Ridge, and Asbury tapped into the Source. The Energy Vortex is similar to the Ethernet cable you use to connect to the internet. The Vortex is a catalyst that when you tap into it catapults you to the place of change that could take a lifetime under your own power.

Think about the Texas oil wells. The oil is flowing underground, unseen, and a powerful resource. Geologists use an instrument known as a magnetometer in searching for the oil. This instrument is used to measure the magnetic field.

The energy.

To tap the main body of oil, you start a new "re-entry" well from the existing well. You don't drill a new well. You utilize the resources already there.

From the channeled messages of Jean Peterson, to the Second Great Awakening of Cane Ridge, the sudden sensation of overwhelming love experienced by Merton, and the glowing chapel of Asbury it's apparent the well is here.

Now in this Age of Aquarius, let us tap into this spiritual energy resource to lead others around the world through the Gates of Higher Consciousness.

Let us use this Kentucky Spiritual Vortex to catapult humanity's level of enlightenment beyond the myths and to Truths of the Cosmos.

Let us tap into this spiritual energy and send it around the globe many times over.

Aeschylus wrote:

"Even in our sleep, pain which cannot forget falls drop by drop upon the heart, until, in our own despair, against our will, comes wisdom through the awful grace of God."

About the Author

An ordained Priest in the Order of Melchizedek, wife, mother, grandmother, and student. This world is not my home, but my school. There are a million and one reasons why I could easily 'throw in the towel' as they say. But I'm not a quitter, and I am praying for you today that love, strength, courage, and hope fill your soul. I feed the birds, sit quietly in a flower garden, marvel at the magnificence of a butterfly, and remind myself, "All is well with my soul."

C. L. Snapp

Contact Information

TapintoKY@gmail.com

Facebook.com/TapintoKY

Available for speaking, exhibits, and events

Photographs may be purchased for a donation of any amount plus $2 shipping within the U.S. for personal use. The images are believed to be blessed and energized for spiritual purposes.

Acknowledgement & Recommended Reading

I have often heard, "save the best for last." So, I did. The following is a just a few of the treasure troves that have guided me down this path and through these woods. Carrying a torch and filling the air with Love and Light. I tip my hat and my heart to them.

💙 Everything "Sleeping Prophet", *Edgar Cayce*

💙 Ruth Montgomery, *"The World to Come" & "Born To Heal"*

💙 Harvey Arden & Steve Wall, *"Travels in a Stone Canoe"*

💙 Eckhart Tolle, *"A New Earth"*

💙 Rev. Daniel Chesbro & Rev. James Erickson, *"The Order of Melchizedek"*

💙 Pete A. Sanders, Jr., *"Scientific Vortex Information"*

www.ingramcontent.com/pod-product-compliance
Lightning Source LLC
Chambersburg PA
CBHW041629220426
43665CB00001B/4